Toothpaste Against Loneliness & Distractions

Nickantony Quach

Copyright (c) 2017 Ri4C.

All rights reserved. All photos Ri4C or otherwise fair use or public domain.

This book is sold subject to the condition that it shall not, by way of trade or otherwise, be lent, resold, hired out, or otherwise circulated without the publisher's prior written consent in any form of binding or cover other than that in which it is published and without similar condition including this condition being imposed on the subsequent purchaser. No part of this book may be reproduced or transmitted in any form or by any means, electronic or mechanical, including photocopying, recording, or by any information storage and retrieval system, without express written permission from the publisher.

Book homepage: Ri4C.com/**TALD**

Contents

Chapter 1 The Unexpected Weekend	1
Chapter 2 Think Toothpaste, Not Weapon	5
Chapter 3 Think Language, Not Machine	9
Chapter 4 Stop Looking for Friends	11
Chapter 5 Start Working on Relations	15
Chapter 6 The Effect of Loneliness on Health	19
Chapter 7 Avoid Phantom Relationships	23
Chapter 8 Move Toward Your Ideals	27
Chapter 9 Competence, Autonomy, and Relatedness	31
Chapter 10 Belonging, Meaning, and Purpose	35
Chapter 11 Navi as Toothpaste Against Distractions	39

1 | The Unexpected Weekend

"I have a new program for myself at 80," mom told me in Vietnamese at the start of October 2022. She lives by herself in another state. "I plan to let go of many things in the house, minimize social interaction, and just enjoy being alive one day at a time. I should get used to living a lonely life. After 45 years of looking, I found no long-lasting friends. Disgusted with looking further for one, I no longer care for socialization."

"We're not robots. What we are apparently is lonely. There is a loneliness epidemic out there; it is widely reported," said Bill Maher on HBO the previous night. "A Morning Consult poll found that almost four out of five young adults consider themselves lonely and have trouble forming relationships outside their home."

During the same weekend, Alec Mustafayev (pictured, right) was upgrading the content of The Dictionary of Thumoslang. Here is a preview of its contents:

Ri4C.com/Shop   Toothpaste Against Loneliness & Distractions

- Othering; that means, social rejection.

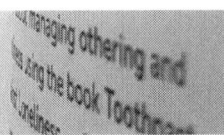

The unexpected weekend alignment of the three events mentioned above led me, Nickantony Quach (pictured, left), to write this book the following days. Mr. Mustafayev joined in and ensured the book was helpful to every cohort.

2 | Think Toothpaste, Not Weapon

Toothpaste is a paste used with a toothbrush to clean teeth. The paste typically delivers fluoride as an active ingredient that helps prevent tooth decay and gum disease. By eight years of age, many children brush their teeth without further help from their parents. Neither children nor parents think toothpaste is a fighting instrument against decay-causing bacteria.

Toothpaste is not a weapon used in combat. Preventing tooth decay does not involve fighting or violence of any kind. The risk of injury, much less death, is zero when not brushing your teeth for a few days.

However, tooth decay comes faster without preventive measures being taken. The consequences of not brushing include stained teeth, tooth decay, gum disease, and long-term health problems such as periodontal disease associated with higher risks of kidney disease, dementia, and certain cancers.

- Devastating; that means, laying waste.
- Violence; that means, devastating force.
- Fight; that means, opposing through violence.
- Tool; that means, a task-based device.
- Instrument; that means, a precision tool.
- Weapon; that means, a fighting instrument.
- Combat; that means, opposing vigorously.

Loneliness is like decay-causing bacteria. It hurts you over a long period, not within a few hours. As a health risk factor, loneliness is more like obesity and smoking. According to Loneliness and social isolation as risk factors for mortality: a meta-analytic review by HoltLunstad, et al., 2015, obesity and smoking lead to the same risk for premature death as loneliness.

You cannot kill loneliness once and for all. You cannot fight loneliness with a weapon used in a single battle. To prevent loneliness, think of using toothpaste, not a weapon. You need to work at it as frequently as you brush your teeth. It's that easy, but it takes time and a lot of perseverance.

- Loyalty; that means, constant support.
- Devotion; that means, purposeful loyalty.
- Adherence; that means, steady devotion.
- Perseverance; that means, unwavering adherence.

Thumoslang is the toothpaste against loneliness; the following pages offer usage and directions. By eight years of age, children should have a foretaste of Thumoslang. It's never too late to learn Thumoslang, but the earlier, the better.

Ri4C.com/Shop   Toothpaste Against Loneliness & Distractions

3 | Think Language, Not Machine

Thumoslang is the toothpaste against loneliness, distractions, and poor performance. The suffix -lang should give it away as a language. Users must think of Thumoslang as a language, not a machine, an app, or anything that can automatically do the work for the user.

Suppose you're a migrant in the United States who does not speak English. "Learn English," a native speaker would suggest. "English helps you save time in your daily life." In that case, it costs you a lot of time to learn the language initially. However, when you are fluent in the language, you will not lose much time in your daily life due to linguistic and social difficulties. Likewise, you must first learn how to use Thumoslang before you can enjoy discharging its power.

To use the toothpaste against loneliness, teach others how to discharge the power of Thumoslang. They will be glad to keep their loneliness at bay. That is how you can help each other start chasing after your ideals as soon as possible and, thus, live a good life.

The first book for beginners to learn Thumoslang is Life in 184 Words, pictured above, also known as Thumoslang on the Run (OTR). The second book for beginners, pictured below, is Thumoslang for Character Renovation (TCR). Learners need them when they take Thumoslang Basic Training Course 102. The course and the two books are available online free of charge.

4 | Stop Looking for Friends

Your friends want you to spend time with them but refrain from passing on any of your judgments to them. Being a true friend is not all fun and games because refraining from passing on judgment takes a lot of undesirable effort. Let's take a closer look at friendship.

First, explore the concept of judgment using the following thumbnail definitions:

- Imposing; that means, applying as compulsory.
- Metrics; that means, standards of measurement.
- Judgment; that means, imposing metrics.

The following thumbnail definitions should clarify the concept of friendship.

- Experience; that means, firsthand knowledge.
- Companionship; that means, the shared experience.
- Friendship; that means, companionship without judgments.
- Friend; that means, a judgmentless companion.

Without passing judgment on you, your friends do not care to change your behavior, the content of your character, or your way of life. Your friends do not want to change or improve you as a person. Your loneliness is not their problem. Friendship gives the concept of peer pressure a lousy reputation.

I've always tried to be a friend to my mom. As her friend, her behavior should always be acceptable to me. My mother should know better; why should I correct her and make her feel bad?

"I have a new program for myself at 80," mom told me in Vietnamese at the start of October 2022. She lives by herself in another state. "I plan to let go of many things in the house, minimize social interaction, and just enjoy being alive one day at a time. I should get used to living a lonely life. After 45 years of looking, I found no long-lasting friends. Disgusted with looking further for one, I no longer care for socialization."

How my mom felt is the result of spending time with friends, one of them being myself. Her friends don't dare to change her ever. Her unhappiness is not due to the lack of friends. She always had friends, but their friendships with her did not last.

Spending too much time with friends wastes your most valuable resource: your time. Spending time looking for friends is even worse.

Rather than looking for friends, there is a better way!

5 | Start Working on Relations

The activity carried out between Mr. Thompson, a teacher, and Sophia, one of his students, is never a relation. The following Thumoslang thumbnail definitions should explain why.

- Service; that means, deliberate assistance.
- Benefit; that means, service to others.
- Usefulness; that means, offering a benefit.
- Value; that means, the level of usefulness.
- Purpose; that means, value to others.
- Involvement; that means, causing inclusion.
- Relation; that means, purposeful involvement.

In the above example, Mr. Thompson's purpose is teaching, which is his value as a service to the student. Sophia's purpose is learning, which is her value as a service to the teacher. She and other students help him keep his job by showing the school they can learn from him.

The teacher and the student service one another. Their activity is not a relation because both participants do not have the same purpose in their shared activity. If two participants in the same activity do not share the same purpose, they provide a set of two services instead of creating a relation between them.

The following examples are not good or bad. They merely demonstrate what a relation is or is not.

- Two students teaching one another are not creating a relation.
  They provide a service to each other.
- Two individuals meeting only for sex have a sexual relation.
  They have the same purpose in the shared activity.
- Two strangers riding the same bus do not have a relation because their purposes for the ride differ.
  One might be on the way to school, the other to a workplace.

Being together does not make a relation. The following example might hit home for many. Two members of the same family might not be creating a relation during a meal if one is doing homework on a laptop while the other watching a TV show. In this case, their hunger acts as the "bus" they ride together. They might share the same table only because they were hungry simultaneously. They did not sit together for the same purpose.

6 | What About Revolutionizing Inner-city

About Revolutionizing Inner-city Classrooms?

"According to U.S. Census Bureau surveys, Americans have been spending less time with friends and more time alone since before the pandemic, which has only intensified the sense of social isolation," states the description of the video [Why Americans are lonelier and its effects on our health]. "Laurie Santos, a Cognitive Scientist and Psychology Professor at Yale University, joins John Yang [on January 8th, 2023] to discuss the health effects of loneliness and what can be done about it."

Below is a transcript of their conversation. The author revised the verbal exchange for clarity.

"People with robust social connections are likelier to live longer, healthier, and happier lives," said John Yang. "But according to Census Bureau surveys, people were spending less time with friends and more time alone even before the pandemic. That only intensified the sense of social isolation and loneliness. Laurie Santos is a Cognitive Scientist and Psychology Professor at Yale University. Her class, Psychology and the Good Life, is one of the school's most popular courses. She's turned it into a podcast, The Happiness Lab. Laurie Santos, how pervasive is this problem in America right now?"

"It's pretty bad; it's often talked about as an epidemic," replied Laurie Santos. "Some surveys reveal that around 60% of people in the U.S right now report feeling lonely regularly. That's pretty devastating from a public health perspective, right? That is worse than rates of obesity. Everything we know suggests that loneliness might be as big of a public health threat in terms of like the effect that it has on our bodies and our minds."

"What's brought this on?" asked Yang. "Why, the pandemic, I think, aggravated it. Even before the pandemic, people were talking about this."

"If you look at rates of loneliness, there's evidence that they've been increasing linearly since the 19 seventies, long before the pandemic," said Santos. "That's long before some other culprits, iPhones, and so on. And so the evidence points to the fact that they're probably many at once. But those things bring us a much more unhappy and isolated population."

"What are some of those causes that are running together?" asked Yang.

"One of the big ones we don't often think about is just time, right? People are busy," said Santos. "People are spending more time at work. We don't have enough free time to connect with the people we care about. There are also lots of other exciting demands on our time. Back in the 1970s, there wasn't Netflix and all these video games and the kinds of things we could do ourselves to entertain ourselves. And I also think this social media wasn't around in the 1970s, but it has a big effect. Our technology and theory are there to connect us socially. How often have you been to a restaurant and seen people not talking to the folks at their table because they were looking down at their phones? We're increasingly connecting through our technology, which means missing out on the connections we can experience in real life."

"What are the health effects of loneliness?" asked Yang.

"There are many surprising [health effects of loneliness]," said Santos. "Individuals reporting feeling lonely are more likely to experience things like dementia, heart disease, and stroke, which affects longevity. Meaning that people who self-report feeling lonely are even more likely to die than those who aren't. Vivek Murphy, the current Surgeon General, estimates that long-term loneliness damages your health, like smoking 15 cigarettes daily."

"It used to be that much of this discussion about loneliness focused on older people," said Yang. Retired people lose that social connection to work, or their spouses or partners may die. But are we seeing this more among younger people now?"

"That's the most striking thing, especially for me as a College Professor, of the current rates of loneliness among our young people," said Santos. "So nationally, among college students, we see levels of loneliness around 60%, which was striking to me. These are young students living on campus, often in the dorms with other students. Yet 60% of them reported feeling very lonely most of the time."

"Talk about that," requested Yang. "They were living in a group situation, yet they were lonely. Are they alone in a crowd?"

"Yeah, I think interacting with their technology prevents connection in real life," said Santos. "I can't tell you how many times I've walked into my dining hall and seen, you know, a crowd of students, each of whom has your big headphones on, looking down at their laptop screens and looking down at their phones. We're missing out on the connection that can happen when you talk to someone in person and have that real-life social connection."

"What can people do to avoid this or if people are feeling lonely?" asked Yang. "What advice do you have for them?"

"The first advice is to remember that it's a common problem," said Santos. "I think loneliness can feel stigmatizing. It can feel like there's something wrong with you if you're feeling lonely. If you realize that, you know upwards of 60% of people out there feel the same. You know, it's not such a bad thing, right? You can admit to it, and I think admitting that you're feeling lonely is part of the first step. I think one thing to do is make sure you're connecting with the folks you have in your life. One of the problems with being busy is that we don't often take the time to connect with people. We care about our friends and family, but it's as simple as picking up the phone to reconnect with them. I think there are also ways that we can try to make new connections. And this is something that I think we often forget to do right again. It's too easy to stay in our house and watch Netflix. But you know, if you're watching the basketball game, could you head out to, you know, a pub and watch that basketball game? Can you join a craft group if you're doing something engaging in knitting or even on a craft? Another big change we've seen since the 1970s is that these so-called third places, where people would meet with other friends, like bowling leagues and so on. These things have gone away in the modern day, but we can bring them back. We can also act to make those kinds of collective social connections."

"Laurie Santos of Yale University," said Yang. "Thank you very much."

"Thanks so much for having me on," said Santos.

7 | Avoid Phantom Relationships

A phantom relationship is a relationship in your mind but not in reality. Phantom relationships are a waste of time. Avoid spending much of it worrying about a nonexistent relationship. Consider the following thumbnail definitions:

- Autonomy; that means, being free from external control.
- Independence; that means, self-sufficient autonomy.
- Relation; that means, purposeful involvement.
- Relationship; that means, ongoing and independent relations.

A relationship requires three conditions:

1. You have at least two relations.
2. The relations must be independent of one another.
3. Each of the relations must be ongoing.

If you have less than two relations in what you believe to be a relationship, it is a phantom relationship. Suppose you are in a Chess Club and have a chess relation with every other member, but outside of the club, you have nothing to do with other members. In that case, none of them are in a relationship with you.

If a relation disappears automatically when you end another one, the former depends on the latter. Suppose you are in a Robotic Club, and all its members attend the same school as yours. When you stop going to school, you must stop interacting with the Robotic Club in school. Any robotic relation would thus disappear automatically. In that case, you cannot count robotics and school as independent relations in any relationship defined by Thumoslang.

One must maintain at least two independent relations in the same relationship to keep it going. To keep a relationship with a classmate beyond graduation, create two ongoing and independent relations outside the school ahead of graduation. Do the same for school friends to minimize fading friendships after graduation.

Thumoslang speakers do not waste time in phantom relationships because they use the above Thumoslang thumbnail definitions to discern consequential from phantom relationships. That is how to do social accounting. You cannot manage relationships without a precise number. Master your relationships, or they will master you.

8 | Move Toward Your Ideals

Your ideals are all the milestones most meaningful to you. They are the Most Important Thing in Your Life. "You must struggle to reach every milestone most meaningful to your life," according to Chapter 11 of Life in 184 Words. "People around you often make it harder for you to do it. Your relationships with them should be considered the social roadblocks in your life. They generate the bulk of the unwanted drama in your social life. The social shortcuts are your relationships with those who make it easier to advance your ideals."

- Social shortcut; that means, faster towards your ideals.
- Social roadblock; that means, slower towards your ideals.

"You can reach your ideals faster by adding more and more social shortcuts while neutralizing more and more social roadblocks in your life. Family and friends tend to be the people who bring both roadblocks and shortcuts to your life. They exaggerate benign events and bring about unwanted drama whenever they act as roadblocks slowing you down in your journey toward your ideals." The phrase your ideals is a shorter way of saying your ideal self, which specifies what you truly want to become. "Everything else is secondary," said Steve Jobs.

- Your ideal self; that means, what you truly want to become.

To move faster toward your ideals, avoid phantom relationships and minimize social roadblocks. Add more and more social shortcuts to your life to reach your ideals as soon as possible.

For an elaboration, watch the video [Start Your Story on Footbridge184 | Footbridge184 | S1E7 | @Ri4CTV].

Alternatively, read Chapter 36, Character Renovation on Footbridge 184, of the book Thumoslang for Character Renovation (TCR).

9 | Inner-city Classrooms

"What kind of experiences do people desire?" asked Herman Narula, CEO of Improbable Worlds Limited, a British multinational technology company founded in 2012. On November 25, 2022, he appeared in the video, [Can the Metaverse Live Up to Its Hype? Tech Leaders Debate | Tech News Briefing Podcast | WSJ].

"The research tells us that they desire fulfilling experiences," said Narula. "They want experiences that give them feelings of competence, autonomy, or relatedness. They want to feel like they can make meaningful choices and relationships with people. If we're going to build a new product, whatever that new product is, if it involves having experiences online, it better provides people more fulfillment than they can otherwise receive through alternatives, including the real world and video games."

- Competence; that means, efficient accomplishment.
- Autonomy; that means, being free from external control.
- Relatedness; that means, frequency of co-occurrence.

The video tells us new products should help people (1) have fulfilling experiences; (2) achieve competence, autonomy, or relatedness; and (3) make meaningful choices and relationships with people.

Competence, autonomy, and relatedness are complex concepts. Many books include several chapters covering just one. Consider the third concept, relatedness. It is a step toward belonging, which is one of the three elements of navi. For an elaboration, see Chapter 9 of the 2022 book Thumoslang for Character Renovation (TCR).

- Belonging; that means, secure relations.
- Meaning; that means, description of importance.
- Purpose; that means, value to others.
- Navi; that means, belonging, meaning, and purpose.

According to TCR's Chapter 9, "a navi is a set of three things: belonging, meaning, and purpose. If you do not have one of these, you do not have a navi. You cannot have a good life without it. You might be on track toward your ideals when you have a navi. Otherwise, without it, there is no hope. You have a navi as soon as you have a sense of belonging, hold up your meaning, and express your purpose."

"Surprisingly, you must not have a relationship to have a sense of belonging. You can have secure relations without having relationships.

If you don't remember the Thumoslang thumbnail definitions for relation and relationship," see New Subject in School, Chapter 9 of the 2022 book Life in 184 Words, also known as Thumoslang on the Run (OTR).

- Relation; that means, purposeful involvement.
- Relationship; that means, ongoing relations.

Relatedness, belonging, and such concepts are what failed joiners in extreme social isolation need to have desperately. David Brooks elaborates in a video uploaded the same day but unrelated to the previously mentioned one.

"This is obviously a problem that is centuries in the making and the first place," said David Brooks in the November 25, 2022 video [Brooks and Capehart on recent mass shootings and the lame-duck session of Congress]. "We are a gun culture. We have a lot of guns in this country, too many guns in this country, so I think that is the primary cause of why this happens in America more than in other places. But it combines with another problem that is at least decades long, which you can call extreme social isolation. Tons of studies have been done on the sort of men who do this sort of thing, and what you find is a culture of complete invisibility. They are unseen at school and around their neighborhoods. One researcher said they are not loners; they are failed joiners. They want to have a social life, but for one reason or another, they cannot have it."

10 | Belonging, Meaning, and Purpose

Thumoslang is the toothpaste against loneliness. "By eight years of age, children should have a foretaste of Thumoslang," claimed Chapter 2. It is never too late to learn Thumoslang, but the earlier, the better. To get started, do the following steps, explained in earlier chapters:

- Stop Looking for Friends (Chapter 4)
- Start Working on Relations (Chapter 5)
- Avoid Phantom Relationships (Chapter 7)
- Move Toward Your Ideals (Chapter 8)

Remember, your ideals are all the milestones most meaningful to you. Together they are your ideal self, which specifies what you truly want to become. "Everything else is secondary," said Steve Jobs.

How do you know that you are on your way toward one of your ideals? The answer is its navi, a set of three things: belonging, meaning, and purpose; see Chapter 9 of the 2022 book Thumoslang for Character Renovation (TCR).

- Belonging; that means, secure relations.
- Meaning; that means, description of importance.
- Purpose; that means, value to others.

You are on your way toward an ideal of yours when you have a sense of belonging, know your meaning, and express your purpose. The difficulty mounts when you count all the milestones most meaningful to your life. You are on your way toward your ideals when you feel belonging, are aware of your meaning, and express your purpose for each ideal of yours.

What should you do if you are alone and not knowing your ideals? The answer is Thumoslang Basic Training Course 102. This course makes you understand the importance of navi. You must deal with more unwanted distractions than necessary without navi for each of your unrealized milestones. Navi is your toothpaste against distractions.

To use the toothpaste against loneliness, teach others how to discharge the power of Thumoslang. After you put them through a slow-burn transformation to become fluent in Thumoslang, they will be glad to keep loneliness at bay for you. That is how they would appreciate you helping them chase after their ideals as soon as possible and, thus, live a good life.

The first book for beginners to learn Thumoslang is Life in 184 Words, pictured above, also known as Thumoslang on the Run (OTR). The second book for beginners, pictured below, is Thumoslang for Character Renovation (TCR). Learners need them when they take Thumoslang Basic Training Course 102. The course and the two books are available online, free of charge.

Ri4C.com/Shop   Toothpaste Against Loneliness & Distractions

What should you do while you are alone and not knowing your ideals? Again, the answer is Thumoslang Basic Training Course 102. Read its Preface and Prologue, then follow the course instruction in every chapter. The course will teach you how to use Thumoslang in your own life, as a toothpaste against loneliness and distractions.

11 | Navi as Toothpaste Against Distractions

Navi is a set of three things: belonging, meaning, and purpose. You are heading toward one of your ideals when you have navi for it. You must have a navi for each of your ideals to have the navi for your life.

- Belonging; that means, secure relations.
- Meaning; that means, description of importance.
- Purpose; that means, value to others.

Belonging, meaning, and purpose are not about personal knowledge but group experience. Developing navi single-handedly is futile as a single person cannot turn a creative prototype into a product of Significance.

To conceive navi as toothpaste against loneliness and distractions, develop a wealth-building friend group. Use bongo siblings as second minds for all you do.

To prepare for building a bongo from scratch, learn to master Thumoslang and renovate your character by taking Thumoslang Basic Training Course 102 (BTC102). Avoid going it alone; involve a few locals in the course as soon as possible. Make others feel more in control.

To expand your bongo, let everyone know how you will volunteer as their champion for personal ideals. To keep in-person friends for life, be their secondmind and support them in developing passive income streams based on their ideals. They can live longer using better healthcare through sustainable wealth.

Nickantony Quach

A resident of Providence, Rhode Island, Nickantony "Nick" Quach enjoys riding a bike around town and meeting people on Thayer Street, a popular destination for students from nearby colleges. This street was where Nickantony taught a 2015 graduate of Brown University the first Thumoslang thumbnail definition ever created; **respect** (on page **65**.) The student used it over the following weeks to effectively wipe out the most recurring, troublesome issues with his parents, as he reported to Nick in an email.

At a city in Texas, 1800 miles away, Nickantony came up with the definition 14 years earlier as the first and only lesson throughout the first grade for his son. He did not intend to use it anywhere else. Until he received the email from his mentee, he did not think much of its potential for widespread effect. Soon after, he nurtured a desire to write about it.

Unexpectedly, less than a year later, Mark Canny met and joined Nickantony with the same desire, but for a much greater cause. In April 2015, the writing began for what would become the book "Thumos: Adulthood, Love, & Collaboration."

Alec Mustafayev

Alec Mustafayev (born 2002) is the second high school student who has ever encountered Thumoslang. Part of this experience is captured in the video, "No Rules", which is Episode 8 in Season 7 of the YouTube series NDBaker93. As a matter of fact, his reaction to Thumoslang is captured by the 20 episodes in Season 7 of NDBaker93.

Alec did not always think of myself as a writer, but had been coming up with creative storytelling ideas for his entire life. By the time he was in his freshman year of highschool, so many of these ideas had added up in my mind over time that Alec felt that needed to put them to use. He self published his first book, **Rebellious**, at the age of 15.

Quach and Mustafayev Group

QMG stands for the Quach & Mustafayev Group, formed in August 2020 by Nickantony Quach (pictured, right) and Alec Mustafayev (left). They and their associates work under the QMG banner. **Scan** the **QR codes** beneath each of them to learn more about them. QMG is the operator of Ri4CTV, a channel on YouTube. Its sister channel on Instagram goes by the same name. The following pages display their various projects.

Novels by QMG

- **Reborn with Power** - The year is 2036. Like most big cities. Washington D.C is a hub for the most revolutionary technology available to the public. Beneath the surface however, lie machines most never see or conceive of. Though only a bystander. Casey Dagher finds herself at the center of a conflict she has no place in.

- **Fountainhead** - Her name was once Casey Dagher. That life was cut short when she was stabbed to death in an alleyway. Miraculously, she survived, but things were different. She gained new abilities; superhuman strength, incredible precision, the product of a mechanical humanoid body she survived in. Reborn with power, Casey, now known as Jaklyn Lionheart, was given a second chance at life as special agent, working on stopping threats with robotic powers like her's from hurting innocent people.

Books by QMG

- Life in 184 Words, aka. Thumoslang on the Run (**OTR**)
    - This book, Life in 184 Words, also known as The Guide to Thumoslang, helps you increase the productivity of your group, advance the progress of your community, and make your own life better. Learn to keep yourself on the shortest path towards your desired life path without needing to put blind faith in parents, religions, or other forces. Using all you learned from them, Thumoslang helps you see what they taught you in a new light.

- Thumoslang for Character Renovation (**TCR**)
    - Using Thumoslang, the author attempts to trace the slow-burn personal transformation of several Thumoslang students. The more you command thumbnail definitions, the more you are fluent in Thumoslang. With this fluency, you can be far more powerful than you have been led to believe. With the science of Thumoslang, people can discover their true capacities through a slow-burn transformation. That is a way to test your power and thereby keep your loneliness at bay for good.

- Trekvella – Thumoslang on Kindle Vella
    - Trekvella is a collection of over eight series covering more than 60 episodes on Amazon's reading platform Kindle Vella. In addition to teaching Thumoslang, most episodes serve as introductions to and a glimpse into the lives of real people with real problems seeking practical solutions. These episodes also maintain a consistent set of main characters who possess an overarching plot among all the one-offs. So far, these characters are Alec Mustafayev, Jairson Ascencao, Norman D. Baker, and Nickantony Quach.

Thumoslang Stories
Nickantony Quach

The Kindle Vella series Thumoslang Stories shows you how to super-power your social life using true stories of Thumoslang's immense power.

Practical Guide to Thumoslang
Nickantony Quach

The Kindle Vella series Practical Guide to Thumoslang shows you how Thumoslang actually works behind each reported social interaction.

Thumoslang at Work
Nickantony Quach

The Kindle Vella series Thumoslang at Work reports true stories of people improving their lives using Thumoslang.

Thumoslang Philosophy
Nickantony Quach

The Kindle Vella series Thumoslang Philosophy offers portrayals of Thumoslang in its most unfiltered form.

Personal Startup Using Thumoslang
Nickantony Quach

The Kindle Vella series Personal Startup Using Thumoslang shows you how to use Thumoslang for your business-of-the-self.

Thumoslang Chronicle
Nickantony Quach

The Kindle Vella series Thumoslang Chronicle tells you about the people and events behind the making of Thumoslang.

Parenting Made Perfect
Nickantony Quach

The Kindle Vella series Parenting Made Perfect shows you how to improve relationships in your traditional family.

The Business of Your Ideals
Nickantony Quach

The Kindle Vella series The Business of Your Ideals shows you how to speed up your ideals and run a professional business using second-mind partners.

Reparenting Trek
Nickantony Quach

The Kindle Vella series Reparenting Trek reports all the critical steps taken by the project whose mission is to reparent humanity.

Services by QMG

- Thumoslang Workshop 401
    - Start Your Story Here is a show Alec and Nick, also known as the QMG Duo, perform in the street. Its mission is to get you started writing The Biggest Story for Your Life. Consequently, Start Your Story Here is another name for **Thumoslang Workshop 401**. The online booklet Start Your Story Here acts as a handout in the workshop. To access it, aim your browser at Foresight Handout, the shortcut link Ri4C.com/Handout.

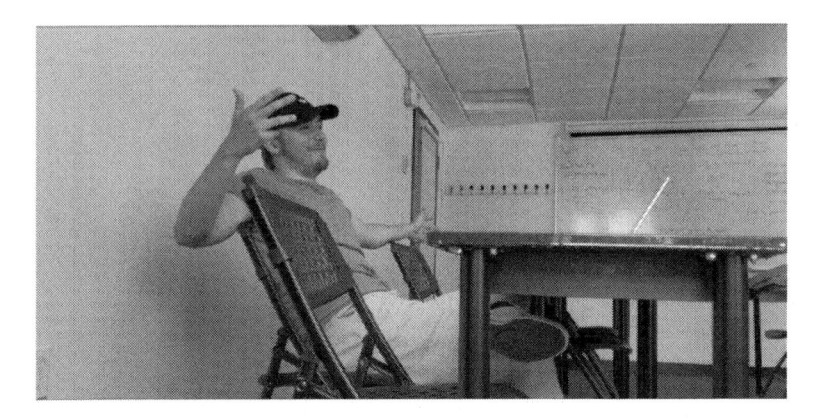

- Footbridge 184
  - **Footbridge 184** is an affectionate name for the ***Ri4CTV Chess & Storytelling Program on the Van Leesten Memorial Bridge***, curated by **Ri4CTV** and sponsored by the Providence Parks Department.
  - Come visit us to **learn chess, enjoy games with friends**, and **tell your story on camera**.
  - Keep up with our **changing program hours** using our **website** or **social media**.

Made in the USA
Columbia, SC
28 February 2023